Messages of

HEALING

for **Lent 2023**

Messages of

HEALING

for **Lent 2023**

3-MINUTE DEVOTIONS

MICHAEL WHITE and **TOM CORCORAN**

Ave Maria Press AVE Notre Dame, Indiana

Nihil Obstat: Reverend Monsignor Michael Heintz, PhD
            Censor Librorum
Imprimatur: Most Reverend Kevin C. Rhoades
            Bishop of Fort Wayne–South Bend
Given at: Fort Wayne, Indiana, on 25 February 2022

Founded in 1865, Ave Maria Press is a ministry of the United States Province of Holy Cross.

www.avemariapress.com

Paperback: ISBN-13 978-1-64680-176-3

E-book: ISBN-13 978-1-64680-177-0

Cover and text design by Samantha Watson.

Printed and bound in the United States of America.

Introduction

We live in a fallen, broken world. Life beats us up and lets us down. Have you ever noticed how many bumps, bruises, knicks, and knocks little kids pick up? It just kind of happens to them. But the same thing happens to us too. Maybe we don't get playground wounds anymore, but in different ways, in each stage of life, we get hurt simply *living* our life. Beyond the physical wounds, we also get wounded emotionally, spiritually, mentally, and relationally.

Some of the wounds are shallow; others go deeper. There are injuries from the past that we still carry today. Some are more recent. Disagreements among friends always hurt, and broken relationships can be traumatic. There is intentional harm done to us as well as harm that is the result of carelessness and thoughtlessness. And, of course, there's the harm that is self-inflicted, resulting from our own poor choices.

We have wounds, and we need healing. That doesn't make us weak. It makes us human. Each human being needs healing on every level of their being. That's why it is so interesting to read through the gospels and consider all the times that Jesus is described as healing people.

In story after story, time after time, we see Jesus the healer. Sometimes the gospel writers give us details about just how the healing took place. Other times, healings are mentioned in passing as if they were a regular feature of his daily ministry. Bringing healing to a hurting world was central to Jesus's mission.

In Matthew's gospel, John the Baptist wants to know if Jesus is the Messiah, the one who was to come. Jesus responds that the proof is in his physical healings: "Go and tell John what you hear and see: the blind regain their sight, the lame walk, lepers are cleansed, the deaf hear, the dead are raised, and the poor have the good news proclaimed to them" (Mt 11:4–5).

In the Gospel of Luke, Jesus explains that he came to heal our emotional and psychological wounds: "The Spirit of the Lord is upon me, because he has anointed me to bring glad tidings to the poor. He has sent me to proclaim liberty to captives and recovery of sight to the blind, to let the oppressed go free" (Lk 4:18). Perhaps most significantly, Jesus described himself as a healer of souls: "Those who are well do not need a physician, but the sick do. Go and learn the meaning of the words, 'I desire mercy, not sacrifice.' I did not come to call the righteous but sinners" (Mt 9:12–13).

Jesus came to heal; he is called the Divine Physician. But that healing doesn't just happen automatically. In fact, over and over again we see that Jesus's healing was resented and even opposed. From the gift of sight to the man born blind and the restoration of wholeness to the man with a withered hand, the religious leaders opposed Jesus when he healed people. They were jealous of his power and the potential it had to change and transform people's lives.

In truth, there are voices that speak against healing in our lives: sceptics who say it is out of reach and naysayers who claim it can't be done. There are people who will actually get in the way of healing to maintain power or for financial gain. We live in a world that is influenced by a spiritual enemy who does not want to see healing take place. There is pride and fear in our own hearts, too, which makes us reluctant to admit our need for healing.

But we do *need* healing because we live in a fallen and broken world. At the same time, our healing will be opposed *because* we live in a fallen and broken world.

We pray that this Lenten prayer booklet will help you meet the Divine Physician, who wants to heal you in a special way this Lent. We further pray that it will help you overcome any opposition that would get in the way of the healing and wholeness Jesus wants you to experience over the next forty days.

Fr. Michael and Tom
Church of the Nativity, Timonium, Maryland

WEEK OF
Ash Wednesday

Wednesday, February 22

Even now—oracle of the LORD—return to me with your whole heart, with fasting, weeping, and mourning. Rend your hearts, not your garments, and return to the LORD, your God, For he is gracious and merciful, slow to anger, abounding in steadfast love, and relenting in punishment.

—Joel 2:12–13

As we begin our Lenten journey with fasting and contrition for our sin, the prophet Joel reminds us of God's character. He longs to extend his grace and mercy to us. He is kind to us and does not wish to punish us for our sins.

Our heavenly Father is better to us than we are to ourselves, especially to our hurts and pains. We do not always treat our hearts and souls with mercy, kindness, and grace. Instead, we get angry that past hurts keep coming back up. We get annoyed at ourselves that we haven't "gotten over it." To experience healing this Lent, we must learn to have the same approach to our hurts and hang-ups as our heavenly Father does.

....

Pray today for the grace to be gracious, merciful, and kind to your own heart and soul. Ask your heavenly Father to teach you to be like him.

Thursday, February 23

[Moses said,] "I call heaven and earth today to witness against you: I have set before you life and death, the blessing and the curse. Choose life, then, that you and your descendants may live, by loving the LORD, your God, obeying his voice, and holding fast to him. For that will mean life for you, a long life for you to live on the land which the LORD swore to your ancestors, to Abraham, Isaac, and Jacob, to give to them."

—Deuteronomy 30:19–20

Moses speaks to the people of Israel as they prepare to go into the Promised Land and he prepares to go home to God. He reminds them that they have a basic choice to make, the only choice we all face: death or life.

When we choose life, we choose healing. God brings healing and life to our bodies and souls. When we refuse to be healed, we choose death to our bodies and souls. Loving God, obeying him, and persevering in a relationship with him is the way of life, healing, and wholeness.

....

Tell God today that you love him and want to obey him and remain in relationship with him.

Is this not, rather, the fast that I choose: releasing those bound unjustly, untying the thongs of the yoke; setting free the oppressed, breaking off every yoke? Is it not sharing your bread with the hungry, bringing the afflicted and the homeless into your house; clothing the naked when you see them, and not turning your back on your own flesh? Then your light shall break forth like the dawn, and your wound shall quickly be healed.

—Isaiah 58:6–8a

The people of Israel wonder why their fasting is not getting them anywhere. They fast, but it does not seem to make a difference in their experience. Speaking through Isaiah, the Lord calls them to act on behalf of people in need. Feed the hungry, clothe the naked, and let the oppressed go free. Then they will see results from their fasting and be healed.

We tend to think of healing as simply passive. This passage from Isaiah teaches otherwise: healing requires action on our part to cooperate with God's grace. God wants us to work with him toward our health, healing, and wholeness.

....

Pray for the grace today to act on behalf of your own health, healing, and wholeness.

Saturday, February 25

Psalm 86:1–2, 3–4, 5–6

Teach me your way, O Lord, that I may walk in your truth.

Incline your ear, O Lord; answer me,
>for I am afflicted and poor.
Keep my life, for I am devoted to you;
>save your servant who trusts in you.
>You are my God.

Teach me your way, O Lord, that I may walk in your truth.

Have mercy on me, O Lord,
>for to you I call all the day.
Gladden the soul of your servant,
>for to you, O Lord, I lift up my soul.

Teach me your way, O Lord, that I may walk in your truth.

For you, O Lord, are good and forgiving,
>abounding in kindness to all who call upon you.
Hearken, O Lord, to my prayer
>and attend to the sound of my pleading.

Teach me your way, O Lord, that I may walk in your truth.

First Week

OF LENT

Sunday, February 26

We know intuitively that something is not right with us. One of the reasons people love watching soap operas, reality TV, or politics (and what are politics and the news but often a real-life soap opera?) is that for a few minutes we can see the wounds or dysfunctions of others, taking the focus off our own. We may have problems, but at least they are not that bad.

Even in our denial and deflection, we often intuitively feel that all is not well in the deepest part of our being. We know there is a wound and that it has hindered us. Having wounds doesn't make us strange or abnormal. They make us human.

We get bruises. We get nicked up. Some of the wounds are small, and we keep going. Some are deeper wounds that stop us in our tracks. Some wounds are from the past that have never really been healed. Some are fresher wounds from recent events.

Life beats us up, but the good news is that Jesus came to heal us. He came to heal our physical, mental, emotional, spiritual, and relational wounds. Our role is to open up our heart and let him heal us.

....

Tell Jesus that you are open to his healing this Lent.

Monday, February 27

The Lᴏʀᴅ God formed the man out of the dust of the ground and blew into his nostrils the breath of life, and the man became a living being.

—Genesis 2:7

Genesis tells us that God created human beings to have intimacy with him. God forms man with his own hands from the clay of the ground. He blows into his nostrils the breath of life. It is God's breath that gives us life and animates us. Our hearts and souls are meant to experience and know the love and care of our Creator. Love is the origin and the destiny of our lives.

God created you to have intimacy with him. Every human being is meant to live in close relationship with him. His breath and life sustain us. In him we live and move and have our being.

....

Thank God, the almighty Maker of heaven and earth, that he wants a personal relationship with you. Thank God that he knows you intimately. He knows your hurts and wounds and still loves you.

Tuesday, February 28

Then the LORD God planted a garden in Eden, in the east, and placed there the man whom he had formed. Out of the ground the LORD God made grow every tree that was delightful to look at and good for food, with the tree of life in the middle of the garden and the tree of the knowledge of good and evil.

—Genesis 2:8–9

God intimately creates human beings and then he creates paradise. Our hearts and souls were meant to live in a life of absolute love and connection with our Creator and with one another. We were created to live in harmony with ourselves. But that's not the world we were born into. Genesis tells us something went wrong.

God's creation is all good. When God had the world as he wanted it, there was no suffering, no sickness, no tears or torture, and no disease or death. Evil is not so much a thing but a choice to turn away from God and his love.

The tree of life represents a choice to depend on God and to live in that connection. The tree of knowledge of good and evil represents a choice to rely on our own wisdom and self-sufficiency. As people with free will, we can always make a choice. When it comes to our wounds, we choose either to invite God in or to rely upon our own resources.

....

Pray for the grace to go to God rather than trust in your own resources when you are wounded.

Wednesday, March 1

But the snake said to the woman: "You certainly will not die! God knows well that when you eat of it your eyes will be opened and you will be like gods, who know good and evil."

—Genesis 3:4–5

The tempter says to the woman that God is holding out on her by telling her not to eat the fruit from the tree of knowledge. The tempter tells us the same things: God is keeping good things from us. If we want to truly find life and a life worth living, we have to run away from God and his one command. He is trying to keep us in the dark about the really good life. Choose to live on your own apart from him and life will be better.

This is the temptation we find over and over again. We are tempted to arrange a life on our own apart from him. Every one of us is tempted to find a life apart from God. We are tempted to deal with our wounds apart from him as well. We are tempted to hide our wounds from God when he is the only one who can heal us.

....

Pray for the grace to overcome the temptation to turn away from God when you are wounded. Ask for the grace to turn toward him when you are injured.

Thursday, March 2

The woman saw that the tree was good for food and pleasing to the eyes, and the tree was desirable for gaining wisdom. So she took some of its fruit and ate it; and she also gave some to her husband, who was with her, and he ate it. Then the eyes of both of them were opened, and they knew that they were naked.

—Genesis 3:6–7

We cannot completely understand the mysterious spiritual principle of original sin and the original wound. Rather than improving their life, eating the forbidden fruit made Adam and Eve aware of their weakness. It brought about a threefold alienation. As a result, we are alienated from God, from ourselves, and from one another. The primary root of our suffering and sickness is separation from God, resulting in the fragmentation of our bodies and souls as well as broken relationships and a broken world.

Every day we feel the effects of original sin. We might do better to call it the original wound, though, which we inherited from our first parents. There is a gaping wound that entered our hearts, our souls, our families, and our world when the first human beings turned away from God, when they chose to eat the forbidden fruit.

....

Like Adam and Eve, we try to hide our wounds from God. Our healing will come from not hiding from God but inviting him into our lives. Tell God today that you are open to him and his desire to heal you through the course of this Lent.

Friday, March 3

> When John heard in prison of the works of the Messiah, he sent his disciples to him, with this question, "Are you the one who is to come, or shall we look for another?" Jesus said to them in reply, "Go and tell John what you hear and see: the blind regain their sight, the lame walk, lepers are cleansed, the deaf hear, the dead are raised, and the poor have good news proclaimed to them."
>
> —Matthew 11:2–5

John the Baptist wonders if he has wasted his life in pointing to Jesus. He is imprisoned, and it looks as if his life will be ending soon. So he sends his followers to Jesus to ask point-blank if Jesus is indeed the Messiah or if someone else is the answer.

Jesus tells John's followers to report back all the healing that has taken place. The blind receive their sight, the lame walk, lepers are cleansed, and the deaf hear. The poor are cared for. These were the signs of the Messiah.

....

Jesus came to heal and restore broken humanity. This was central to his mission as the Messiah. Jesus came to heal and restore you. Invite him into your heart. Ask him to heal what needs to be healed.

Saturday, March 4

Psalm 119:1–2, 4–5, 7–8

**Blessed are they who follow the law of the
  Lord!**

Blessed are they whose way is blameless,
  who walk in the law of the LORD.
Blessed are they who observe his decrees,
  who seek him with all their heart.

**Blessed are they who follow the law of the
  Lord!**

You have commanded that your precepts
  be diligently kept.
Oh, that I might be firm in the ways
  of keeping your statutes!

**Blessed are they who follow the law of the
  Lord!**

I will give you thanks with an upright heart,
  when I have learned your just ordinances.
I will keep your statutes;
  do not utterly forsake me.

**Blessed are they who follow the law of the
  Lord!**

Second Week

OF LENT

Sunday, March 5

Throughout this Lent, we are looking at the fact that we all have wounds. God created us to live in a perfect world of love, but we live in a fallen and broken world. We experience physical, mental, emotional, relational, and spiritual wounds.

We know from psychological and neurological research that these wounds become permanently stored in our brains and every cell of our bodies. Our brains record our experiences, and when probed, our brain remembers every perception and feeling associated with those experiences. Even when not conscious, these memories influence our thoughts, actions, and behavior until they are healed.

....

Jesus came to heal us of our wounds. Today, ask Jesus to show you what wounds he wants to heal in you this Lent.

Monday, March 6

Jesus took Peter, James, and John his brother, and led them up a high mountain by themselves.
—Matthew 17:1

Jesus had many people who followed him. Crowds were always coming to him. And there were other disciples that followed him and supported his work and ministry. Then there were the Twelve Disciples, and within the Twelve, Jesus had a special relationship with Peter, James, and John. They had a deeper, more intimate relationship with Jesus than anyone else. Here, Jesus takes them up the mountain to pray with him. He wants to reveal something about himself that cannot be shared with the crowds, these three disciples, or even the other disciples.

When he walked the earth, Jesus was limited in whom he could give his time and energy to, but because he ascended into heaven, now you can enter into an intimate relationship with Jesus. Jesus wants you to be his intimate ally and to know him more and more.

....

Pray today for a close friendship with Jesus. Pray for the grace to know him more and more. Thank the King of kings that he wants to be your friend.

Tuesday, March 7

And he was transfigured before them; his face shone like the sun and his clothes became white as light. And behold, Moses and Elijah appeared to them, conversing with him. Then Peter said to Jesus in reply, "Lord, it is good that we are here. If you wish, I will make three tents here, one for you, one for Moses, and one for Elijah."

—Matthew 17:2–4

As they were up on the mountain, Jesus became transfigured. His face and clothes shone bright like the sun. Jesus no longer looked like an ordinary man. In this moment, his divinity shone through for Peter, James, and John to see. In addition, Moses and Elijah, the two greatest prophets of the Old Testament, appeared to validate Jesus's identity.

This event, the Transfiguration, parallels the Passion. In both cases, Jesus invites Peter, James, and John with him to pray. In both cases he climbs a mountain. In both cases he is lifted up between two men: Moses and Elijah in the Transfiguration and two criminals at his crucifixion.

The Transfiguration was meant to encourage the faith of Peter, James, and John before the crucifixion. Jesus gave them this mountaintop experience to prepare them for future suffering. In the same way, we get to experience mountaintop experiences so that when we are hurt, we do not forget the goodness of God.

Pray for the grace to remember the goodness of God when you are experiencing hurts and wounds.

Wednesday, March 8

While he was still speaking, behold, a bright cloud cast a shadow over them, then from the cloud came a voice that said, "This is my beloved Son, with whom I am well pleased; listen to him."
—Matthew 17:5

As Peter is talking, God the Father interrupts him. Since Peter was always interrupting others and speaking out of turn, it is appropriate that now God interrupts him. The Father affirms that Jesus is his beloved Son. Jesus is indeed divine, and the Father is well pleased with him.

This is the second time the Father expresses his pleasure and delight in Jesus. The first time came at his baptism before Jesus launched his public preaching, teaching, and healing. Now in the middle of his work, the Father affirms and encourages his Son. Here, he affirms Jesus in front of his closest friends, so not only does Jesus hear the words of encouragement but also they do.

Then the Father gives these instructions to the apostles, so simple and so vitally important: "Listen to him."

....

Take one minute to simply listen to Jesus and what he wants to say to you.

Thursday, March 9

Then from the cloud came a voice that said, "This is my beloved Son, with whom I am well pleased; listen to him."

—Matthew 17:5

Listening to Jesus brings about our healing. So what are you listening for?

You are listening for *what* Jesus wants to heal. Right now you are primed for a certain kind of healing that Jesus wants to give you. Listen for what that is. You may already know what they are, but say, "Jesus, I think you want to heal my marriage." Or "Jesus, I think you want to heal me my heart from careless words." Or "Jesus, I think you want to heal my body." Ask Jesus if that is what he wants to heal. And then listen in your heart.

Then ask *how* he wants to heal you. Maybe Jesus is leading you to receive counseling, journal, forgive someone who hurt you, or tell your story to someone. Or maybe he just wants you to be reminded of his love.

How do you know if it is Jesus speaking? Well, Jesus is always kind and merciful. His words might be challenging, but they are never critical or condemning. His words are going to build you up. They are always accepting of you. The more you listen, the better you will be at hearing from him.

Take a moment to listen to Jesus now. Say, "Give me ears to hear and eyes to see what you are revealing. Let me hear no other voice but yours, Jesus."

Friday, March 10

Yet it was our pain that he bore, our sufferings he endured. We thought of him as stricken, struck down by God and afflicted, but he was pierced for our sins, crushed for our iniquity. He bore the punishment that makes us whole, by his wounds we were healed.

—Isaiah 53:4–5

Six hundred years before Jesus came, the prophet Isaiah was given a vision into the future of a suffering servant. The suffering servant would bear the pain of our offenses. He would be stricken, struck down, afflicted, pierced, and crushed to make us whole. By his wounds we would be healed.

You can listen to Jesus because he intimately knows the truth of your wounds. He felt the wounds of physical pain as nails were driven into his hands and feet. He felt the emotional wounds of abandonment from his friends and of rejection from the crowds. He felt the mental wounds of knowing he was going to die. He felt the spiritual pain of the sins of the whole world on his shoulders. Yet he bore the pain out of love for you. Jesus can give you wisdom and direction because he both suffered all your wounds and overcame them through his resurrection.

....

Reread the verses above from Isaiah. Thank Jesus that he suffered so you might be healed.

Saturday, March 11

Psalm 103:1–2, 3–4, 9–10, 11–12
The Lord is kind and merciful.
Bless the LORD, O my soul;
    and all my being, bless his holy name.
Bless the LORD, O my soul,
    and forget not all his benefits.
The Lord is kind and merciful.
He pardons all your iniquities,
    he heals all your ills.
He redeems your life from destruction,
    he crowns you with kindness and compassion.
The Lord is kind and merciful.
He will not always chide,
    nor does he keep his wrath forever.
Not according to our sins does he deal with us,
    nor does he requite us according to our crimes.
The Lord is kind and merciful.
For as the heavens are high above the earth,
    so surpassing is his kindness toward those who
        fear him.
As far as the east is from the west,
    so far has he put our transgressions from us.
The Lord is kind and merciful.

Third Week

OF LENT

Sunday, March 12

God created us to live in a perfect environment of love—but we live in a fallen and broken world. We experience physical, mental, emotional, relational, and spiritual wounds.

We have looked at two steps for our healing. The first is simply to be open to it. We have to accept that we need healing, and we have to be open to the healing Jesus wants to bring into our lives. Last week, we looked at a second step: listen. Jesus wants to heal the wounds in our lives, but we have to listen to him. We have to listen for *what* he wants to heal in us and *how* he wants to do it.

This week, we are going deeper and probably taking the most difficult step. It will take some strength of will to take this step. You have to be tough. This is the surprising thing about healing: it takes some mental and emotional toughness to find it. We tend to think of healing as soft, but it is not soft. It is kind and caring, but healing also requires strength of will.

....

Pray for the grace and strength you need to take the next step to find healing.

Monday, March 13

[Jesus] came to a town of Samaria called Sychar.
. . . Jesus, tired from his journey, sat down there at
the well. It was about noon.
    A woman of Samaria came to draw water.
Jesus said to her, "Give me a drink." . . . The
Samaritan woman said to him, "How can you, a
Jew, ask me, a Samaritan woman, for a drink?"
                                                —John 4:5–9

Jesus and the disciples are traveling in the heat of
the day. They stop to take a break by a well. Jesus is
tired from walking and sits down to get some rest
and water. A Samaritan woman comes to the well
to draw water for herself and her household. Jesus
has no bucket, so he asks her for a drink.

In doing this, Jesus broke two huge societal
conventions. First, men did not talk to women in
public. Second, Jesus is a Jew, and she is a Samaritan. Jews and Samaritans didn't talk to one another.
The Jewish people regarded Samaritans as half-
breeds as they had intermarried with Gentiles and
had adopted pagan practices. The Jewish people
looked down on the Samaritans, and the Samaritans
hated the Jewish people for looking down on them.

....

Take a moment to realize there is nothing about you
Jesus does not accept—no matter who you are. Jesus
loves and accepts you regardless of your past failures
or mistakes. Thank Jesus for this great love. Pray for
the grace to not allow barriers to get in the way of a
deeper relationship with Jesus.

Tuesday, March 14

[The woman] said to him, "Sir, you do not even have a bucket and the well is deep; where then can you get this living water? Are you greater than our father Jacob, who gave us this cistern and drank from it himself with his children and his flocks?" Jesus answered and said to her, "Everyone who drinks this water will be thirsty again; but whoever drinks the water I shall give will never thirst; the water I shall give will become in him a spring of water welling up to eternal life."

—John 4:11–14

Jesus promises the woman some water, but he doesn't even have a bucket to use at the well. The woman points this out and then she says something very ironic. She asks Jesus if he is greater than Jacob.

Jesus maybe smiled here. Maybe he thought, *Yes, I am superior to Jacob.* But rather than saying it outright, he speaks to the woman about the living water. He says, "Jacob provided you with a well, but you have to keep coming back to the well to quench your thirst. It is something outside you. I want to give you something that will dwell within you—something inside you that I will provide." Jesus is talking about the Holy Spirit. He is talking about putting God's life in our souls so we can access it at any time. While our bodies thirst for water, our souls thirst much more for God.

....

Pray for the living water of the Holy Spirit to come into your life.

Wednesday, March 15

The woman said to him, "Sir, give me this water, so that I may not be thirsty or have to keep coming here to draw water."

—John 4:15

Jesus has said he can give this woman water that will quench her thirst. He means giving the Holy Spirit, but she thinks he is speaking about physical water. So she responds, "Give me this water so I don't have to come back to this well anymore."

The woman at the well had arranged her life around her pain. She has come to the well at noon. Most women went to the well early in the morning to avoid the heat and so they would have water throughout the day. Wells served as a place of community to come and connect. But the Samaritan woman goes out of her way to avoid people.

With Jesus's offer, she sees a way forward. She sees a way to get water, to avoid coming at the hottest part of the day *and* to avoid all the people in the town. She sees a way to make her life easier without getting to the root cause of her pain.

....

Wounds will tempt us to go out of our way to avoid facing them. Is there a wound you have been avoiding? Or are there some people you go out of your way to avoid because they remind you of that wound? Pray for Jesus to come into that wound.

Thursday, March 16

Jesus said to her, "Go call your husband and come back." The woman answered and said to him, "I do not have a husband."

—John 4:16–17a

Ouch. That would have stung. When Jesus mentioned her husband, the woman would have immediately felt pain. She answers that she does not have a husband. In fact, she has had five husbands, which means five men have rejected her.

You know how you say something and accidentally hit a nerve? The person you're talking to tries to make it sound as if it's not a big deal, but you witness the instant change on their face and in their voice. They are trying to dismiss it and move on. That's exactly what the woman is doing here.

But Jesus does not move on. He doesn't let it go because he is after her healing, and unless she faces the pain she feels over her former relationships, she will not be healed. Most of us don't want to acknowledge these intense feelings of pain from our wounds. We believe if we acknowledge the pain, we will remain stuck in our pain and loneliness. However, the truth is that Jesus loves us enough to enter into our pain with us.

....

Thank Jesus that he loves you enough to help you face the pain of your wounds. Pray, "Jesus, I give myself to you now to be my healer. I give you my wounded heart. I invite you into the broken places in my heart. You know my brokenness, and you love and accept me anyway. Come and speak to me here."

Friday, March 17

Jesus answered her, "You are right in saying, 'I do not have a husband.' For you have had five husbands, and the one you have now is not your husband. What you said is true." The woman said to him, "Sir, I can see that you are a prophet. . . . I know the Messiah is coming, the one called the Anointed; when he comes, he will tell us everything." Jesus said to her, "I am he, the one who is speaking with you."

—John 4:17b–19, 25–26

Jesus calls out the brutal facts. The woman has had five husbands and now is living with a man who is not her husband. This would have made her a social outcast. Only men had the right to divorce. In that society, women needed a husband or some other man for protection and the basic necessities of life. So here is this woman's pain. She has lost all these men, and now she is rejected by the rest of the townspeople. Jesus exposes her pain.

In hearing Jesus uncover her life, the woman sees he is someone special. He can read her heart. And then in saying the Messiah is coming, she is almost asking him, "Are you the one? Are you the Messiah?" She has seen that Jesus knows all her flaws and her pain and still loves and accepts her.

....

Jesus reveals himself to be our Savior and Messiah when we let him into our wounds. Pray, "Jesus, I give myself to you now to be my healer. You know my brokenness, and you love and accept me anyway. Come and speak to me here."

Saturday, March 18

Psalm 51:3–4, 18–9, 20–21ab

It is mercy I desire, and not sacrifice.

Have mercy on me, O God, in your goodness;
>   in the greatness of your compassion wipe out
>   my offense.
Thoroughly wash me from my guilt
>   and of my sin cleanse me.

It is mercy I desire, and not sacrifice.

For you are not pleased with sacrifices;
>   should I offer a burnt offering, you would not
>   accept it.
My sacrifice, O God, is a contrite spirit;
>   a heart contrite and humbled, O God, you will
>   not spurn.

It is mercy I desire, and not sacrifice.

Be bountiful, O LORD, to Zion in your kindness
>   by rebuilding the walls of Jerusalem;
Then shall you be pleased with due sacrifices,
>   burnt offerings and holocausts.

It is mercy I desire, and not sacrifice.

Fourth Week

OF LENT

We experience physical, mental, emotional, relational, and spiritual wounds. These wounds can be wounds of omission, which are the result of being overlooked or neglected, such as not being understood or nurtured, not receiving appropriate boundaries or discipline or feedback, or not being cherished or delighted in. Or these wounds can be wounds of commission that come from the bad things that happen to us. They are what we typically think of as traumatic events. Scientific research tells us these wounds become permanently stored in our brains.

Healing is key to living happier, healthier, more successful, and more significant lives. Healing, though, is not just about us. As we seek healing we will have a better impact on the people around us. Hurt people hurt people, and we have all been hurt. Healed people heal people.

So far we looked at three steps for healing. The first is simply to be open to our need for healing. The second step is to listen to Jesus and what he wants to heal in us. The third is to take perhaps the hardest step of entering into and confronting our wounds. However, we do not this on our own. We invite Jesus in to heal our broken hearts, minds, and souls.

....

Pray this week for the grace to do what Jesus wants you to do so you participate in your own healing.

Monday, March 20

As [Jesus] passed by he saw a man blind from birth. His disciples asked him, "Rabbi, who sinned, this man or his parents, that he was born blind?"
—John 9:1–2

The gospel writer John does not give much context for this story; however, Jesus and the disciples must have some knowledge of the man's past because they knew he had been born blind. The disciples ask whose fault it is that this man is blind. Clearly, they thought, either he or his parents did something wrong. How, you might wonder, could he have done anything wrong if he was born blind? But in fact some rabbis taught at this time that you could sin in the womb.

That was the thought of the time: if something bad happened to you, then you must have done something wrong or deserved it. At times we can fall into the same erroneous thinking. Often the reason we don't want to admit our wounds is because in the back of our minds we think we did something wrong or we somehow deserved them. Certainly there are some wounds that are self-inflicted, and our healing will come from taking responsibility for them. But many of our wounds are not our fault. Someone did something to us intentionally or unintentionally.

....

Pray for the grace to know that most of your wounds are not your fault. Pray that in accepting this truth you will open you to experiencing Jesus's healing.

Tuesday, March 21

Jesus answered, "Neither he nor his parents sinned; it is so that the works of God might be made visible through him."

—John 9:3

The apostles ask who sinned, and Jesus answers that no one is personally to blame for this man's blindness. His blindness is not a punishment from God but just the opposite as God will now take this wound, this physical problem, and use it for good. God's work and power will be made visible and plain through this man. This will be a sign that Jesus really is sent from God.

Healing a blind man was an incredibly important sign for people in that time and culture to show them that Jesus was really the Messiah. Six hundred years earlier, the prophet Isaiah had foretold that when the Messiah came he would open the eyes of the blind. Healing was to be core to the mission of the Messiah, so seeing Jesus's power to give sight to the blind and heal was very important for that generation. But it is important for our time and generation too. When we experience Jesus's power through healing, we become more convinced in our hearts that Jesus is our Savior and Messiah.

....

Pray today that the works of God may be made visible in your life. Ask God to heal you or others so that you may see his work.

Wednesday, March 22

When he had said this, he spat on the ground and made clay with saliva, and smeared the clay on his eyes, and said to him, "Go wash in the Pool of Siloam" (which means Sent). So he went and washed and came back able to see.

—John 9:6–7

Why did Jesus spit on the ground, make clay, smear it on the man's eyes, and then tell him to wash it out?

Each of Jesus's healings is personal and unique because we all need different medicines. This detail emphasizes the personal nature of Jesus's healing but also references Genesis 2:7, which tells us that God made human beings out of the dust of the ground. In alluding to this verse, John is saying that Jesus is the Son of God who was present at creation, and just as God created human beings from dust, Jesus makes us a new creation.

Up until this point, Jesus had taken all the initiative. The man born blind had done nothing to participate in his own healing until he chose to follow Jesus's instructions and wash off the mud. Jesus wants us to participate in our own healing. He wants to partner with us as we bring God's grace, love, and mercy into this world, starting with our own healing. God wants to bring his love and grace to us, but he does not do so without our consent. He wants it to be our choice.

....

Pray for the grace to know what Jesus wants you to do to participate in your healing.

Thursday, March 23

When Jesus heard that they had thrown him out, he found him and said, "Do you believe in the Son of Man?" He answered and said, "Who is he, sir, that I may believe in him?"

—John 9:35–36

The man born blind washes the mud out of his eyes and can see. Eventually the man born blind is brought to the religious authorities for their opinion and interpretation of the miracle. However, because the authorities are so blinded by their hatred and envy of Jesus, they refuse to believe he performed the miracle. When the man born blind refuses to change his testimony and not lie to them about how he was cured, the religious leaders throw him out of the Temple.

After the man born blind is thrown out of the Temple, Jesus presents himself to him. This is the first time he has seen Jesus, and the man born blind does not know that the person who stands in front of him is the same one who healed him. So Jesus asks him if he believes that the person who healed him is truly the Messiah. Will he trust his life to the man that healed him?

And the man born blind says yes. Tell me who he is. I want to know.

....

Jesus asks us if we want more than healing, if want to know him. Beyond healing us, Jesus wants a personal relationship with us. Pray for the grace to know Jesus and go deeper in your personal relationship.

Friday, March 24

Jesus said to him, "You have seen him, and the one speaking with you is he." He said, "I do believe, Lord," and he worshipped him.

—John 9:37–38

Over the course of probably a couple of hours, the man born blind moves from having no relationship with Jesus to having a superficial knowledge of him and then to understanding he is the Son of God and worshipping him.

Whatever our healing, it is going to bring us deeper in our relationship with Jesus. He is what we need. He gives us himself. He heals us because he loves us. True healing of our bodies, hearts, and souls cannot come apart from him.

"Go and wash" were the instructions Jesus gave to the man born blind. The man participated in his own healing once he went and washed the mud on his eyes. Jesus tells you today to go and do something. What is that "something" for you?

Maybe it is "Go and forgive." Maybe it is "Go and confess your sins because your wound is self-inflicted." Maybe it is "Go and journal." Or "Go and find counseling." We cannot be healed apart from Jesus, but he will not heal us without our participation. Healing requires that we seek it out and do something on our behalf or on the behalf of others.

....

Ask Jesus to show you what action step he wants you to take so you can be healed.

Saturday, March 25

Psalm 23:1–3a, 3b–4, 5, 6

The Lord is my shepherd; there is nothing I shall want.

The LORD is my shepherd; I shall not want.
　　In verdant pastures he gives me repose;
beside restful waters he leads me;
　　he refreshes my soul.

The Lord is my shepherd; there is nothing I shall want.

He guides me in right paths
　　for his name's sake.
Even though I walk in the dark valley
　　I fear no evil; for you are at my side
with your rod and your staff
　　that give me courage.

The Lord is my shepherd; there is nothing I shall want.

You spread the table before me
　　in the sight of my foes;
you anoint my head with oil;
　　my cup overflows.

The Lord is my shepherd; there is nothing I shall want.

Only goodness and kindness follow me
　　all the days of my life;
and I shall dwell in the house of the LORD
　　for years to come.

The Lord is my shepherd; there is nothing I shall want.

Fifth Week

OF LENT

Wounds are part of life because we live in a broken world. The question is not "Do we have wounds?" because we do. The question is "What do we do with those wounds?" Ultimately, we have two choices. We can choose to turn to God and invite his healing into our lives. Or we can try to deal with our wounds apart from him. Since we have been made for relationship with God, we really only find true healing by turning to him.

Over the course of this devotional, we have looked at ways to invite God into our lives to heal us. First, we have to be open to Jesus healing us. Second, we listen to Jesus and see what he wants to heal in us. Third, we enter into the wound and invite Jesus into it as well. Fourth, we need to act. We go and do what Jesus tells us to do. Healing isn't passive. It's active. Healing requires something from us.

....

This week in our prayer we will look at God's timing in our healing. Pray today for the grace to be in rhythm with his timing.

Monday, March 27

So the sisters [of Lazarus] sent word to him, saying, "Master, the one you love is ill." When Jesus heard this he said, "This illness is not to end in death, but is for the glory of God, that the Son of God may be glorified through it."

—John 11:3–4

The sisters of Lazarus are Martha and Mary. They send word to Jesus through a messenger that his close friend Lazarus is sick. They describe him as the one Jesus loves. In other words, they are begging Jesus to come do something to help Lazarus by reminding him of their close relationship.

Jesus's response seems to be positive. He says the illness is not to end in death. He seems to indicate that Lazarus is going to get better. Then he adds that the illness will be used for God's glory.

God never wastes a hurt or a pain. He wants to use it for his glory. That sounds as if God needs the spotlight. But we are meant to rely on God. We can't have healing apart from him because there is no real life apart from him. When people are healed through Jesus, they come to know that he is the Son of God. People come to realize that he has been sent by God to bring God's love and grace to the world. Our hurts and hang-ups are opportunities for God's great love to be revealed to the world.

....

Pray that God will use healing in your life to reveal his love for others.

Tuesday, March 28

> Now Jesus loved Martha and her sister and Lazarus. So when he heard that he was ill, he remained for two days in the place where he was.
> —John 11:5–6

These two sentences together don't seem to make sense. Jesus loves Martha and her sister, Mary, and yet he delays.

When you hear someone is sick, you go and see them. But Jesus stays behind two days. Jesus at other times had healed strangers and went out of his way to do it. It seems as if Jesus does not care about Lazarus suffering and the suffering of Martha and Mary. He seems indifferent to their hurts.

Sometimes Jesus seems indifferent to our hurts and pains. He doesn't act as quickly as we would like. In those times, we can doubt God's love. God's love, though, is constant, even if we do not see it.

Sometimes God is delayed because his will is being opposed. Sometimes God is delayed because he is disobeyed. God gave free will, and so sometimes his will is not done immediately. Sometimes God's response feels delayed because he has another purpose. He is working out something else in us. He is building our trust in him or our character or perseverance.

....

Pray today for the grace to trust in God even when there are delays in healing or seeing him act.

Wednesday, March 29

When Jesus arrived, he found that Lazarus had already been in the tomb for four days. . . . Martha said to Jesus, "Lord if you had been here, my brother would not have died. [But] even now I know that whatever you ask of God, God will give you."
—John 11:17, 21–22

People handle grief and loss and pain in different ways: Martha goes out to meet Jesus; Mary stays at home. Martha is an active person, a doer. Mary is the more reflective person. Some people handle wounds, loss, and disappointment by getting busy. They deal with the pain by being active. Other people withdraw into themselves.

Martha is blunt and direct with Jesus, telling him that he could have done something about Lazarus's illness. "Jesus, if you had been here, my brother would not have died. So you are to blame, Jesus, for his death."

She expresses her grief with anger. Do you know you can get angry at God? He can take it. Often we are afraid to voice our disappointment about him to him. We think we have to hide it from God. But if you feel angry with God, go ahead and let him know it. If you feel he has let you down, tell him. In the psalms, David did this all the time. He would yell at God and express his hurt that God wasn't coming to help him.

....

Share with God today how you are feeling about your life and circumstances.

Thursday, March 30

> Jesus said to her, "Your brother will rise." Martha said, "I know he will rise, in the resurrection on the last day." Jesus told her, "I am the resurrection and the life; whoever believes in me, even if he dies, will live, and everyone who lives and believes in me will never die. Do you believe this?"
>
> —John 11:23–26

Jesus tells Martha that her brother will rise. She says she knows that he will rise at the end of time. The Jewish people believed in resurrection. Resurrection means more than that. It means you will get a new body—a resurrected body that will join again with your soul.

Jesus says he is the resurrection. He conquers and overcomes death. So if we believe in his resurrection, then we also believe that pain, suffering, hurt, and even death do not have the final word. Our hurts, hang-ups, and even death can be overcome. If Jesus rose from the dead, then your wounds don't have the final say over you.

The question becomes, do we believe that? If we believe that to our core, it doesn't mean we won't get wounded or suffer loss. But we believe we can recover from that loss. We believe God will bring good from the loss.

....

Pray today for the grace to believe in the power of the resurrection to overcome all your wounds and to provide healing.

Friday, March 31

> So Jesus . . . came to the tomb. It was a cave, and a stone lay across it. Jesus said, "Take away the stone." Martha, the dead man's sister, said to him, "Lord, by now there will be a stench; he has been dead for four days." Jesus said to her, "Did I not tell you that if you believe you will see the glory of God?" So they took away the stone. . . . The dead man came out, tied hand and foot with burial bands, and his face was wrapped in a cloth. So Jesus said to them, "Untie him and let him go."
> —John 11:38–41a, 44

Practical Martha protests that there will be a stench. They can't move the stone. Rather than anticipating something life changing, she is concentrating on something small—the smell. How often do we find ourselves focusing on the small problems or rehearsing past grievances rather than trusting that God may bring about something new?

God has a purpose for your pain and wounds. What others intend for bad or what mistakes you have made, God can use for good.

After they remove the stone, Lazarus comes out of the tomb. Now that he is alive again, Jesus tells them to unbind him. Healing is ultimately about unbinding you from the things that are keeping you back: the hurts and hang-ups that keep you from being the person you want to be and what God want to do through you.

....

Pray for the grace to look beyond the smaller hurts and pains of your life to the larger story of God mercy and healing.

Saturday, April 1

Jeremiah 31:10, 11–12abcd, 13

The Lord will guard us, as a shepherd guards his flock.

Hear the word of the LORD, O nations,
    proclaim it on distant isles, and say:
He who scattered Israel, now gathers them together,
    he guards them as a shepherd his flock.

The Lord will guard us, as a shepherd guards his flock.

The LORD shall ransom Jacob,
    he shall redeem him from the hand of his conqueror.
Shouting, they shall mount the heights of Zion,
    they shall come streaming to the LORD's blessings:
The grain, the wine, and the oil,
    the sheep and the oxen.

The Lord will guard us, as a shepherd guards his flock.

Then the virgins shall make merry and dance,
    and young men and old as well.
I will turn their mourning into joy,
    I will console and gladden them after their sorrows.

The Lord will guard us, as a shepherd guards his flock.

Sixth Week

OF LENT

Sunday, April 2

As we enter Holy Week, we will be looking at chapter 53 from the prophet Isaiah. Six hundred years before Jesus came, Isaiah prophesied of a suffering servant. Ironically, he predicts that people will not recognize the suffering servant even after his prediction, that the suffering servant would not be believed to be God's servant. Since Jesus grew up as an ordinary human being, many people dismissed him. He was in so many ways ordinary: a carpenter from the backwater town of Nazareth. He did not occupy a position of power or prestige.

....

Take a moment to thank Jesus for coming as an ordinary human being. He can identify with your ordinary daily routines because he lived them himself.

Monday, April 3

He was spurned and avoided by men, a man of suffering, knowing pain, like one from whom you turn your face, spurned, and we held him in no esteem. Yet it was our pain that he bore, our sufferings he endured.

—Isaiah 53:3–4a

Through his Passion, Jesus knew our suffering and pain. He knew what it was like to be rejected by others. He was rejected by the crowds as they cried out, "Crucify him!" He was hated by the religious leaders who arranged for his death. He was abandoned by his closest followers and friends. He was spurned and held in no esteem.

By the time he was on the Cross, he had been so beaten and bloodied that it was difficult to even look at him. Many had to turn away from him because his face became so disfigured from the beatings. And yet he suffered not because of what he did but because of what we did. He bore the pain and suffering for our sins.

Thank Jesus today that he bore your pain for your sins.

Tuesday, April 4

We thought of him as stricken, struck down by God and afflicted, but he was pierced for our sins, crushed for our iniquity. He bore the punishment that makes us whole, by his wounds we were healed.

—Isaiah 53:4b–5

Jesus went to the Cross and was beaten. As people watched Jesus undergo the Crucifixion, many believed God was punishing him for something he had done wrong. Isaiah prophesied six hundred years earlier that he was pierced for our sins, crushed for our iniquity. *Iniquity* is not a word we use much, but it means gross injustice or wickedness. It is the gross behavior we sometimes choose to do that disgusts even us. Jesus was crushed for our iniquity.

He bore the punishment that makes us whole. By his wounds we are healed. He suffered that we would be made whole, that we would be healed. The best way we can thank Jesus for that gift is to receive it. We invite him into our hearts and souls to heal us and make us whole.

Today, invite Jesus into your heart to heal you.

Wednesday, April 5

We had all gone astray like sheep, all following our own way; but the LORD laid upon him the guilt of us all.

—Isaiah 53:6

Isaiah acknowledges that all of us have gone astray like sheep. We have chased after things that are opposed to God. Unlike sheep, which wander off because they don't know any better, we are culpable and guilty for chasing after sin.

We are culpable for our sins, but we do not have to bear the guilt of our sins. God placed the burden of our guilt on his Son when he placed the Cross on his shoulders.

Jesus bore the burden of our guilt. The best way to thank him for that guilt is to give it to him. We confess our sins, admit our failures, repent, and change, but we do not have to hold onto our guilt.

....

Thank Jesus that he has borne your guilt. Pray for the grace to give it to him and walk in the grace of his mercy.

Thursday, April 6
Holy Thursday

Though harshly treated, he submitted and did not open his mouth; like a lamb led to slaughter or a sheep silent before shearers, he did not open his mouth. Seized and condemned, he was taken away. Who would have thought any more of his destiny? For he was cut off from the land of the living, struck for the sins of his people.

—Isaiah 53:7–8

Jesus went to the Cross like a lamb led to the slaughter. He did not open his mouth or complain about his suffering. He was seized, condemned, and taken away to his death. After his death, people thought it was the end of him. All his preaching and teaching and miracles seemed for naught. He was dead. He was cut off from the land of the living.

But we know that Jesus's death was not the end. While he was struck down for our sins, he would rise again.

....

Thank Jesus that he quietly went to his death so you could live.

Friday, April 7
Good Friday of the Passion of the Lord

He was given a grave among the wicked, a burial place with evildoers, though he had done no wrong, nor was deceit found in his mouth. But it was the LORD's will to crush him with pain. By making his life as a reparation offering, he shall see his offspring, shall lengthen his days, and the LORD's will shall be accomplished through him.

—Isaiah 53:9–10

Jesus is nailed to the Cross and then placed in a tomb. He had done nothing wrong. During his trial, Pontius Pilate says over and over that he found no guilt in him. Jesus is sentenced to death even though he is innocent. Yet it was God's plan. The Father offered his Son as a sacrifice for all of humanity. The Son willingly sacrificed himself so that reparation could be made for our sins and failures.

We are the offspring of Jesus's sacrifice. It was God's will to make us his sons and daughters through the death of and resurrection of his Son.

....

Thank God today for the sacrifice he made for you. Ask God what you can give in return for his sacrifice.

Saturday, April 8
Holy Saturday

Psalm 31:2, 6, 12–13, 15–16, 17, 25

Father, into your hands I commend my spirit.

In you, O LORD, I take refuge;
    let me never be put to shame.
In your justice rescue me.
Into your hands I commend my spirit;
    you will redeem me, O LORD, O faithful God.

Father, into your hands I commend my spirit.

For all my foes I am an object of reproach,
    a laughingstock to my neighbors, and a dread
        to my friends;
    they who see me abroad flee from me.
I am forgotten like the unremembered dead;
    I am like a dish that is broken.

Father, into your hands I commend my spirit.

But my trust is in you, O LORD;
    I say, "You are my God.
In your hands is my destiny; rescue me
    from the clutches of my enemies and my
        persecutors."

Father, into your hands I commend my spirit.

Let your face shine upon your servant;
    save me in your kindness.
Take courage and be stouthearted,
    all you who hope in the LORD.

Father, into your hands I commend my spirit.

Fr. Michael White and **Tom Corcoran** are coauthors of the bestselling Rebuilt Parish series, including the award-winning *Rebuilt*—which led to the CatholicTV series *The Rebuilt Show*, which they host—*Tools for Rebuilding*, *Rebuilding Your Message*, and *The Rebuilt Field Guide*. They also are the coauthors of *Seriously, God?* and the bestselling Messages series for Advent and Lent. They have spoken at conferences and parishes throughout the United States and Canada, and at diocesan gatherings and conferences in Austria, Australia, Germany, Ireland, Poland, and Switzerland. They have been guests on EWTN, CatholicTV, Salt + Light Television, and numerous Catholic radio programs.

churchnativity.com
rebuiltparish.com
rebuiltparish.podbean.com
Facebook: churchnativity
Twitter: @churchnativity
Instagram: @churchnativity

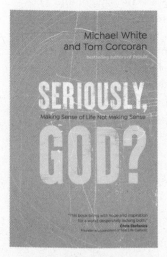